HOW TO HAVE A SUCCESSFUL RELATIONSHIP/ MARRIAGE

An Introductory Guide to Having Your Dream Relationship

Jason Legend

Copyright ©2019 by NJHbooks

All rights reserved, including the right to reproduce this book or portions thereof in any form

ISBN: 9781688992368

DEDICATION

This book is dedicated to my lovely wife, who puts up with more from me than she probably should

CONTENTS

INTRODUCTION

Marriage is a union between two people. Gone are the days where the wedding was simply a union with no other binding factor other than customs and tradition. Today, marriage is legal as the law and law enforcement recognize it. Marriage is one of the things most people (although this is changing) dream of. In fact, if you sample the plans of 100 persons randomly, you will find that 50% of them have "getting married to the ideal partner" as a dream goal.

Often, we are sold the narrative that marriage cures loneliness, gives us constant sexual satisfaction, and makes us pass the unconscious exams given to us by society. These are some of the reasons why people get into marriage. However, marriage is a complicated thing. Yes, this is not to scare you (if you are single), but marriage requires a lot of hard work and input. If you are already married, I'm sure you can attest to this.

Given the amount of work required to make a marital union successful, it's no wonder several persons fail to make a success of their marriage. This is not to say a successful marriage is devoid of drama and conflict: far from it, battles are vital to the growth of a relationship. Strong friendships and relationships are easy to achieve. What you and your partner need are simple strategies, rules, secrets, and critical essentials that will make your relationship blissful.

Luckily for you, most of the helpful tips on marriage and relationships have been compiled in this book. The journey is going to be an interesting and insightful one.

CHAPTER 1

7 REASONS FOR THE RISE IN DIVORCE CASES

50% of marriages in the US end in divorce, so it's no surprise that many millennials are no longer fancy to the idea of getting married. Many millennials prefer to have children outside the bonds of marriage, and several others stay as live-in couples without ever getting married.

Many marriages fail because of partners who are unwilling to put in the effort to make it work, resulting in divorce. Others have to endure unhappy marriages for long periods, hanging on only because of the kids, finances, or societal pressure.

Couples and intending couples must discover the reasons for failed marriages, so they know how best to overcome the challenges. Here are some ideas that lead to the high rate of divorice.

THE GENERAL OPINION THAT MARRIAGE IS DISPENSABLE

Welcome to the 21st century, an era where people are accustomed to a quick fix for almost everything. This culture explains the increase in gambling, lottery, and Ponzi schemes. It explains why self-help authors who sell nothing but lies, become best-selling authors. The truth is that the modern society, most of it, sees anything requiring work to be stressful.

Sadly, our relationships are a victim of this quick fix mentality with many persons going into bonds, believing it's a solution to all their problems. Many persons have character issues that need work. They assume they can waltz into marital life with those issues expecting their partner to keep up - after all, it is love.

Therefore, it comes as no surprise that divorce is on the rise as a lot of married people are not ready to work on themselves and their relationship. Everybody goes into the marriage hoping for the best, but success in marriage requires work.

SELFISH BELIEF SYSTEMS

A lot of persons today are of the school of thought that

propagates the "self-happiness" theme. "Do not stay with a man or woman who is no longer making you happy." "If leaving the marriage will make you happy, better start filing for that divorce right away." In truth, these messages are beneficial. However, it overlooks the need for endurance and sacrifice.

There is an unbalanced side to the "staying happy" movement and applying it blindly opposes the success of most marriages. Regardless of what you might have heard, the fact that a marriage is not working at a particular point in time does not automatically mean you file for divorce. Unions are designed to be life-long commitments, and you don't just call it off whenever you wish to.

Entering a marital commitment means you are prepared to enjoy the good times and endure the bad times while working to make things better. Marriage is a serious institution; it is not *Netflix & Chill*.

A HIGH RATE OF INDEPENDENCE AND LOW RATE OF INTERDEPENDENCE

The society is filled with independent men and women, most of whom have used the virtue of independence to achieve success in their careers. However, many make the mistake of carrying that mindset into marriage.

Marriage is a union with two people, and it demands the input of these two people. Marital problems require cooperation, communication, and synergy, but many people don't recognize this fact. Several partners do not give to the idea of interdependence. Instead, they act insecure whenever their partner tries to help in their area of weakness, which could breed resentment and jealousy. This unwillingness to synergize is a leading cause of divorce among couples.

A little humility and willingness to admit fault goes a long way in preventing divorce among couples.

OVERLOOKING AN ESSENTIAL ASPECT OF MARRIAGE – FRIENDSHIP

The titles' husband' and 'wife' make some people believe their partners are on some form of pedestal; when in truth, the reverse is the case.

When people marry, they frequently forget that their partner should be their friends. If you marry primarily for sex or romance, don't be surprised your marriage ends almost as soon as it began. You will discover the beauty and abs you married for, fade quickly.

If you don't treat your partner like a friend, several aspects of your marriage will fail, and several persons are oblivious to this fact. In the process of their bliss in ignorance, their relationship with their partner becomes estranged and rocky. If most divorcees saw their partner as a friend instead of a person put on a pedestal (that is unattainable), their marriages would never have failed.

LACK OF SELF-AWARENESS

Despite the instant availability of resources and mind-blowing technology in the world, it is ironical how several persons have a scant idea of who they are. This fact may seem shocking, but it's the truth. Many persons jump on the bandwagon of marriage without first understanding why they need to get married. Instead, they align with whatever option is available or what their family thinks is ideal for them. Consequently, they end up married to the wrong person.

People who lack an understanding of self, find it hard to talk about their needs as they are ignorant of what is best for them. Marriages fail for people with this problem. Unfortunately, there are many people like this in modern society, and with that, an increase in divorce cases.

GETTING MARRIED FOR THE WRONG REASONS

A fact often ignored by most people is that the basis for a marriage is a prophecy or determinant of its end. If you get married for the appropriate reasons, and your marriage has the potential to turn out blissful. However, if you marry for the wrong reasons, the chances are high that you would eventually divorce your partner.

Sadly, many people get into marriage for lots of wrong reasons. When you take a sample of the reasons people get married, you will be shocked at why you will hear. The most common reason for getting married revolves around societal pressure, and the victims of this are often, women.

Often, women are put under due pressure from their parents or family to marry (especially when approaching late 20s). This societal absurdity has misled many women, pushing them into marriages they should never have entered. Consequently, such unions turn disastrous with cases of incompatibility.

LOSS OF INTIMACY

Marriages that end in divorce often show a downward

slope in affection while still in form. Like it or not, sex and intimacy are two components of marriage that can't be ignored. Many couples make the mistake of relegating intimacy in their marriage as it advances, and the result is a gradual buildup of tension and apathy. In the long run, such couples have no choice but to call quits.

When sex becomes less regular and unsatisfying, problems are bound to arise in marriages – real or imagined. These problems come in many forms: affairs, emotional unavailability, estrangement, and anger.

CHAPTER 2

5 MYTHS ABOUT MARRIAGES AND RELATIONSHIPS THAT YOU NEED TO STOP BELIEVING

Our beliefs play a massive role in our individual lives. Many a time, our beliefs predate us, stemming from our families and societal backgrounds. We must identify which beliefs we hold that might prove dangerous in the relationship with our partners. Many relationships are at the brink of collapse because of unhealthy belief systems the individuals hold onto. Sadly, many persons mistake these opinions/myths for the fact and go all out defending it.

We must identify these myths/unsubstantiated beliefs as this is the only way we can break from the harm they pose.

What are some of these myths?

SEX IN MONOGAMY GETS BORING OVERTIME

A popular myth is that over time, sex between couples

get boring since it's with the same person. However, this is far from the truth. By keeping the sex life varied, couples can keep it interesting, maintaining the profound satisfaction that comes from sexual intimacy.

Some couples hold this belief blindly, and put in little or no work in their sex life, making a myth a self-fulfilling prophecy. A loss of intimacy takes the spark away from the relationship, resulting in more severe problems.

Do not buy into this myth about relationship sex. If you find yourself in a typical situation, cooperate with your partner to resolve the issue. Keep in mind that emotional openness and the ability to express acts of love are essential in sexual intimacy.

SUCCESSFUL COUPLES DO NOT ARGUE

Another misconception about marriages and relationships is that couples who have a happy relationship do not argue. "Look at them; they don't argue at all. Why can't we be like them?" Individual partners might find themselves telling their partners this. It's not their fault to have fallen victim to this misconception. After all, this is what the media portrays.

Whenever we see a couple smiling and having fun, it's

easy to believe they never have conflict. This misconception makes many persons believe conflicts are detrimental to the success of a relationship. However, in reality, the opposite is true.

Miscommunications and conflicts are bound to occur in relationships. If you see a relationship where the partners don't argue at all, you can rest assured there's much insincerity in it. Absence of conflict means emotional compromises have been reached, and the ripple effect of such an agreement includes trust issues and feelings of disdain.

Therefore, we should disregard the myth that healthy partners do not argue. If you are a single and intending to date or marry, expect arguments to occur in your relationship. However, note that healthy arguments are typically made in lowered voices. The goal of a healthy argument is not to dominate each other. It's to resolve your issues.

PERSONALITY DIFFERENCES HURT RELATIONSHIPS

Here is another common belief, one you must have heard several times. "Date someone who you are compatible with; marry someone who has the same interests as you. If they do not share similar interests with you, they are not your ideal partner." We've heard all these myths painted as the truth. Unfortunately, many of us fall for the falsehood perpetrated by this myth.

In truth, compatibility is an essential feature of any relationship. However, differences do not translate to failure in marriages. What causes the problems is how we respond to these differences. We shouldn't consider the differences as something strange but rather an exciting aspect of the relationship.

Whenever your partner says something or brings a suggestion, you don't necessarily have to accept their opinions (especially if you don't agree with them). Just as well you don't have to spend time looking for fault in what they suggest. You should examine their idea and suggest whatever you feel works best.

YOUR RELATIONSHIP WITH YOUR TRUE LOVE IS AUTOMATICALLY DEVOID OF ISSUES

The true love concept is one of the biggest misconceptions in society. Social media, movie industries, and news platforms continually promote the narrative that true love exists. They also propagate the misconception that if you are in a relationship with your true love, you two should find it easy to work out your relationship. This myth has led many people to destroy their relationships unknowingly.

The truth is that there is nothing like a destined partner or a magical relationship. There is no perfect partner who will know all your needs without you voicing them out in the first place.

If you want your partner to become your "true love," you should learn to communicate. Communication and readiness to listen will make you and your partner desirable to each other. It would be best if you also learned to put your relationship first. Get the misconception of having the perfect partner out of your head. Instead, accept your partner for who they and try your best to develop each other.

FOR A COUPLE TO BE A HAPPY, THEY MUST DO EVERYTHING TOGETHER

If you want to have a successful relationship or marriage, you should remove the belief that you and your partner have to be together at all times. No doubt, quality time with your spouse is a significant relationship booster. However, moderation is key.

While spending time together is helpful, having personal space is more vital for the success of any marriage or relationship. Spending too much time together as a couple does the exact opposite of what you expect it to achieve. It stiffens your productivity and drains you. In the long run, this adversely affects the relationship. If you don't support your partner in the pursuit of their different interests, it will brew estrangement, which will eventually tear down the marriage.

CHAPTER 3

SIGNS OF A SUCCESSFUL RELATIONSHIP/MARRIAGE

Every romantic relationship has the magical, good, bad, and even, ugly times. Marriage is not always all butterflies and paradise. There will be times where you and your partner will get into endless arguments. There will be times where you will keep doubt if he/she is truly the one for you, and there will be times you feel like giving up on the relationship.

It is normal for you to experience the high, mixed, and low phases in relationships. However, it is crucial that you recognize the signs of a successful marriage. The knowledge of these signs will either reassure you or make you realize how much work you have to put into the relationship.

Below are the few vital signs of a successful marriage.

EACH PARTNER HAS THEIR SPACE

An indicator of a healthy relationship is one where partners can enjoy their personal space without having to feel guilty. A relationship where both partners enjoy the quality time together; but, somehow respect each other enough to allow themselves to pursue these dreams is a healthy one.

Space in the relationship fosters closeness, and although it may seem paradoxical, that's the reality. It doesn't mean the love is any less than it should be. Couples who give each other space tend to grow better individually and as a unit.

PARTNERS HAVE SAME CORE VALUES

Couples must have a similar core value system; this will encourage growth. People in a healthy marriage often share specific similar values, from which they draw out their relationship values. Relationship values are critical for the state of the relationship.

A CONSIDERABLE LEVEL OF INTIMACY

Closeness is necessary for a marriage. If couples want to be happy, there must be a reasonable level of intimacy between them. While sex is important, sex is not what makes up intimacy. Intimacy is the familiarity, companionship, sarcasm, and the other adorable things about love that every human desire. A healthy relationship is one where the couples enjoy good times in and outside of the bedroom.

NO SECRECY BETWEEN PARTNERS

If you find out that you feel the constant need to keep things from your spouse, it shows that your communication is poor. This is a good sign that something needs to be done about it.

Successful couples don't keep things from each other. Openness makes couples grow closer and more comfortable with themselves.

CONFLICTS ARE HANDLED IN A CONSTRUCTIVE AND MATURE MANNER

One sign of a healthy marriage or relationship is that couples handle disputes among themselves maturely and constructively. Conflict is a fundamental part of any relationship; it is bound to happen. Hence, having conflicts at intervals does not mean a relationship is not healthy, or it is going awry.

When conflicts occur, couples in healthy relationships don't create drama from it but rather state their positions respectfully so as not to hurt their partner. Such couples also recognize the need to apologize to their partners whenever they are in the wrong.

CHAPTER 4

REQUIREMENTS FOR A SUCCESSFUL RELATIONSHIP/MARRIAGE

Whenever the wealthy people in society are asked for the secret of their success, they point to certain rituals, values, or factors that contribute to their success continually. What this shows is that there are certain ingredients required for success to take place. The same applies to relationships.

For every relationship, there are certain requirements for success, and knowledge of these things goes a long way in helping to create a successful relationship. Successful couples know that the key to success in their relationship goes beyond material possessions. Therefore, they have learned the significance of investing in their efforts in the following six ways.

COMMITMENT & LOVE

Love is beyond the feeling of butterflies you get when you see someone you care about. Love involves a conscious decision to stay committed to a particular person through thick and thin. If there's no love in a relationship, conflict is bound to arise. This happens especially when the source of attraction such as money, looks, or achievements are no longer there or relevant.

As long there's love in your relationship, it is bound to overcome whatever challenge is thrown at it.

FORGIVENESS & PATIENCE

If you want to experience a happy relationship, you are going to need a lot of patience. It would be best if you also had a forgiving spirit. There will be many times when your partner's actions will get on your nerves or push you to the wall. However, successful couples realize that there must be patience and forgiveness in the relationship for it to succeed. These are prerequisites that cannot be ignored.

TIME INVESTMENTS

Time is everything. What people, especially new couples, do not realize is that no relationship can work out without investing time into it. Many persons are engrossed in career pursuit to the extent where we abandon one of life's greatest gifts, the love of our partner.

Quantity and quality time are pertinent if you want to have a successful relationship- the two work hand-in-hand. Your relationship with your spouse is not like any relationship you will have in life. It is more in-depth. Therefore, you must invest enough time in your relationships to make it deep and intimate.

COMMUNICATION

Communication is probably the most critical requirement on the list. Relationship books, podcasts, YouTube videos, and relationship counselors hammer on the importance of communication in successful relationships. There is no lie in this. Partners in successful marriages communicate regularly not only about sharing expenses; they also chat about seemingly mundane things like how their day went.

Communication is indisputably an essential prerequisite on the list as it lays for the foundation of different helpful marriage concepts such as patience, love, among others.

HONESTY AND TRUST

If you desire to have a successful marriage, you should

never forget the vital essential principles of honesty and trust. Honesty is the best policy- the truism of this parlance extends to your relationship and marriage. Honesty and trust lay the best foundation to build your marriage.

Unlike the other prerequisites, honesty and trust do not develop overnight. They require time. Especially trust, this is a virtue that can take years to build. You should also apply carefulness in making sure that you don't break your partner's trust in you. Once broken, it is a hundred times harder to regain confidence.

SELFLESSNESS

In a selfish world, selflessness is a virtue and is responsible for the success of relationships. Most marriages end in shambles because of selfishness whether it is because of infidelity, unwillingness to commit, lack of communication and the likes, everything all points down to selfishness.

Naturally, humans are selfish, but for the sake of your relationship, you should reduce this nature as it's only by doing so that the relationship can become successful. Rather than spend time chasing material things, investing in your relationship to ensure its success will make you happy in the long run.

CHAPTER 5

TIPS FOR HAVING A SUCCESSFUL MARRIAGE/RELATIONSHIP

For every successful relationship, there have been years of conflict, commitment, caring, and friendship behind it. Enjoying a lasting partnership today is almost becoming a dream. However, you and your partner will stand out from the majority if you follow certain principles.

RENEW YOUR COMMITMENTS AS OFTEN AS YOU CAN

One way to have a successful marriage is to treat commitments with the utmost respect. For long term relationships, loyalty is a crucial indicator of success. The level of involvement in a marriage will determine its potential longevity. Couples who want their marriages to last, and have the fairy tale ending of "happily ever after" should decide to remain in the relationship. Commitment means choosing to stay in a relationship with someone, notwithstanding the ordeals.

Recommit to your partner as often as possible. Be faithful to your promises and prioritize your marriage above anything else. Through this, you and your partner are laying the foundation for a long-lasting and happy relationship.

HAVE PLAYTIMES WITH YOUR PARTNER

As adults, we can feel awkward whenever we are tempted to play. In the long run, being uptight spoils the fun that comes with being in a relationship. You must learn to be a playful person if you want a lasting relationship. Having fun as a couple is the right prediction for closeness and satisfaction, and it is evident that closeness and comfort are critical contributors to intimacy.

TALK OUT YOUR CONFLICT

Learn the art of being flexible with the way you handle conflicts. Be direct and oppositional to your partner in your talks whenever you two are experiencing severe disputes. Research shows that being candid in talking out issues with your partner is far more helpful than any approach. On the other hand, be affectionate when your partner tends to get defensive or probably when the conflict is a minor one.

DISPLAY ACTS OF LOVE TO YOUR PARTNER

One tip for having a successful relationship is by showing acts of love to your partner. Humans are social and emotional beings who require validation and love.

In long-term relationships such as marriages, it can be found wanting as routines inescapably become a part of the couples' daily life. Lack of love is one of the factors that kill lots of relationships. If you are short of ideas on how to go about displaying love, try experimenting with new and exciting things with your partner. No matter how foolish your thought might be, it will build bonds between you and your spouse.

You can also show acts of love by paying compliments and performing small gestures that will undoubtedly produce happier partners.

LEARN TO LET GO

One of the significant causes of divorce is the inability of people to let things go. Most people have the "my way or the highway" mentality. This mentality affects their relationships as they tend to escalate matters beyond proportion. For instance, research conducted back in 2013 observed that more than half of the interviewed divorcees ended their marriages due to minor issues that escalated into big fights.

If you want peace and happiness to reign in your marriage, you should learn to take things less personal and let things go. Not only will this approach reduce the frequency of conflicts, but it would also add happiness to a relationship. Always take the high road whenever your partner wants to escalate minor fights beyond proportion.

CONCLUSION

Marriages and relationships are not easy to build as they are dyadic interactions. Do not rely on the information given here alone. Try your best to read more books and watch videos on relationships. Also, the tips given in this book are not conclusively guaranteed to make your relationship a successful one. Every relationship has its quirks. So, not all methods are universal. If you find it hard to make sense out of your marriage or relationship despite your efforts, get an expert.

www.ingramcontent.com/pod-product-compliance
Lightning Source LLC
Chambersburg PA
CBHW051427250726
48655CB00003B/1271